A THOUGHT-PROVOKING BOOK
OF COMMON SENSE

GUN

TALK

THOMAS H. WARD

GUN TALK

A Thought-Provoking Book of Common Sense

By Thomas H. Ward

ISBN-10: 0-9982869-0-7
ISBN-13: 978-0-9982869-0-7

First Edition 2016 Transcendent Publishing

Transcendent Publishing
PO Box 66202
St. Pete Beach, FL 33736
www.transcendentpublishing.com

Transcendent
Publishing

Printed in the United States of America

DEDICATION

This book is dedicated to the thousands of military people and non-military who have served this country since it was founded. Especially to those unknown heroes who gave the ultimate sacrifice during the American Revolution. What brave men they were.

It is also dedicated to the men and women in blue and all law enforcement officers who put their lives on the line every day to protect our freedoms. Without them our country would be in serious trouble. Thank you for your service.

CONTENTS

"In every truth there is non-truth, in every fiction there is non-fiction."

—Thomas H. Ward

A NOTE FROM THE AUTHOR

I had just finished writing this book when I suddenly realized that it was July 2, 2016. Two more days and it would be the Fourth of July. I stopped what I was doing, turned on the History Channel and there it was, the story of the American Revolution; I watched it to completion. What a wonder it is how our country came about. I am an avid student of American History. If you don't know history, then you are bound to repeat the mistakes of the past.

As I watched the American Revolution unfold in front of me on TV, I was spellbound. Then, something occurred to me. The first battles were at Lexington and Concord, Massachusetts. I wondered, who were these brave men? A militia force of 400 that stood against the King's Army, the most feared force on earth at the time. Who were these new American Patriots? Who were these heroes that dared to defy the orders King George, and risked their lives in doing so?

They were nobody and they were everybody, from the farms and small towns of the new America. They were the everyday people: farmers, shop-keepers, blacksmiths, and

ministers … they were Americans like us.

God Bless America, Land of the Free, and Home of the Brave.

INTRODUCTION

Gun Talk is a book of short action-suspense stories. These fictionalized stories are based on real-life self-defense situations that people have been put into through no fault of their own. These Americans had to defend themselves because no one, not even the police, could help them. The stories provide a scenario asking, *what would you do?* **Read the stories and find out what it feels like to be helpless and at the mercy of deadly criminals.**

Interwoven in between the real stories are comments about gun rights. Most importantly, there are summaries of four past terrorist attacks committed in the United States. Read the summaries and see if you can find out what these four attacks all have in common. It will shock you how most of these attacks could have been prevented. It will blow your mind that our most respected law enforcement agency knew who these terrorists were and even interviewed them. Why and how did this happen? This is discussed later in the book.

The terrorist incidents were put in this book because we are talking about gun control. Guns were used to kill United States citizens. You will find out why it is important to analyze these terrorist events. The news media doesn't always tell the whole story.

Whether you are a new gun owner, a life-long NRA member like me, or even an anti-gunner, this short book provides something for everyone. The book provides support to clarify the debate once and for all about whether people should own guns and the meaning of the Second Amendment.

The 2ND Amendment: *"A well regulated Militia, being necessary to the security of a free State, the right of the people to keep and bear Arms, shall not be infringed."*

What does this mean? The wording has created considerable debate about the intended scope and meaning. The interpretation has been twisted from its original meaning by modern-day attorneys. Attorneys use the definitions of words from modern-day dictionaries, while using modern-day logical thinking, and try to apply this to define the Second Amendment.

The Second Amendment is a lot more than words. It is a type of thinking. It is a rational judgment made by free men that started long ago, before this country was founded. It came into full meaning at the battles of Concord and Lexington. This is discussed and explained later in this book.

Most people do not really understand why or how the American Revolution started. Most people don't know how the war with Great Britain came about. Most people don't know what the final straw was that broke the camel's back, which caused bullets to fly and the American Colonists to split away from Britain. This information will also be discussed.

Do we need gun laws? Yes, but we already have thousands of them. Should everyone own a gun? No, not everyone, that goes without saying. Should some types of guns be banned? Machine guns and sub-machine guns are already banned unless you have a Federal Permit to own one. Has the government dropped the ball in protecting the home front? Yes, it appears that is the case. The preceding points will be reviewed in further detail later.

Near the end of this book, there is a Gun Selection Guide for beginners. Purchasing your first gun can be a confusing shopping experience since there are so many types of guns. This book explains what new buyers should know before going to the gun store.

At the very end of the book is a copy of the "BILL of RIGHTS." These are the first Ten Amendments of the United States Constitution. Please take the time to read them.

PART ONE

SELF-DEFENSE

STORIES and COMMENTS

Read the following four stories, and then ask yourself, what would you do?

THOMAS H. WARD

STORY ONE
"THE KEY WEST TRIP"

After a long weekend in Key West, Florida the Jones family decided to drive back to Tampa early Monday morning to beat the rush hour. Mr. and Mrs. Jones, along with their two daughters, Amy and Erin, are on this short vacation trip.

They had a great time in Key West, taking a much needed break from work and college. They didn't want to leave so early, but had to get on the road by 4 am to beat the rush hour in the Miami area. Mr. Jones had made this trip many times over the last eight years that they had lived in Florida. Visiting Key West for a long weekend every few months was a great stress reliever.

Checking out of the hotel at 3 am, they headed north on the only road out of the Keys, Route 1. Mr. Jones was driving while the rest of the family was asleep. He knows the way by heart and takes Route 1 to Interstate 75, which crosses the southern tip of Florida known as Alligator Alley. It is named this because Route 75 passes through the Everglades swamp, which is the natural home for gators.

Alligator Alley is a desolate straight strip of highway that extends from Miami to Naples and is approximately 130 miles long. It takes about two hours to cross. The problem with this stretch of road is that there is only one rest area, which is located halfway across. Cell phone reception is not possible for most of the way. There are emergency road phones every few miles in case someone breaks down. The State Highway Patrol covers this highway and is supposed to make regular patrols across it looking for stranded motorists and speeders.

This Interstate is pitch-black at night. There are no street lights or ambient light from the city once you're a few miles into Alligator Alley. Mr. Jones is driving at the speed limit which is 70 mph. Actually, his car won't go much faster than this. He's a safe driver and doesn't want to break the speed limit or take any risks with his precious family in the car.

When they finally reached Alligator Alley it was almost 5 am. The sun would be coming up soon. Jones was happy about that because he didn't like driving in the dark. No one else was on the road, either behind him, or coming from the other direction. He sat back and relaxed, putting on cruise control, listening to music, while his wife and daughters slept. Everyone was tired from the long weekend of swimming and diving. He guessed they would be home by noon, if everything went well.

What worried Jones most was getting a flat tire out in the middle of nowhere. If you're sitting on the side of the road, you are at the mercy of any nutcase who comes along. It is also possible that a blowout could cause you to lose control of the car and you end up in a ditch, in the gator infested swamp. He once read a story about a man who was eaten by a gator after his car crashed along Alligator Alley.

Jones popped open a coke and thought, *I'll be happy once we reach Naples where some people actually live.* He glanced in the mirror and saw a car speeding up behind him. Its bright lights were on but so were his. It's dark out here and you never know what could be in the road. He had heard stories about gators lying in the road. If you hit one of those big critters, anything could happen.

Suddenly, catching him off guard, the car zoomed up behind him. It got right on his bumper and started flashing its bright lights on and off. Jones didn't know what to do, so he slowed down thinking it might be a cop. The car behind him also slowed down, still flashing its bright lights. Jones slowed down to 40 mph and the car was still right on his bumper.

He knew if it were a cop he'd have some flashing police lights, so Jones sped up and put the pedal to the metal. When he did this, his wife and daughters woke up and asked what was going on. He told them what the car behind them was doing. Everyone turned around in their seats to look at it.

One of his girls said, "Dad, please don't stop! I'm scared."

He replied, "Don't worry, I'm not stopping."

Mrs. Jones asked, "What do they want?"

"I don't know. Maybe they want to rob us or something. But I'm not stopping to find out."

Jones floored the car and hit a top speed of 80 mph. He said, "Damn, I can't go any faster. I can't out run them."

His wife yelled, "Slow down or you'll get us all killed," as she held on to the dashboard with both hands. Jones quickly glanced over at his wife. He could tell she was terrified. He took a quick look in the mirror at his daughters who sat there wide-eyed. Their faces told him they were really shook up.

The car stayed right on their tail flashing its bright lights, so Jones slowed down, back to the speed limit. The car zoomed around and pulled up next to them. Two crazy looking men stuck their heads out of the window and yelled, "Pull over and stop!"

Amy, the oldest girl, said, "Look at those nuts!"

Erin replied, "I don't want to look at them." She ducked down and covered her eyes. "We're gonna die!"

"Don't' worry. We're not going to die." Jones reassured his family.

Then the car passed them and moved in front of the Jones' car. Its brake lights came on and it started to slow down. Jones couldn't out run them and they knew it. Now they were stopping him in the middle of nowhere. He scanned the highway looking for another car. There were none. He thought, *where's a cop when you need one?*

Mr. Jones guessed what these guys were going to do. They would bring him to a stop. Surround his car and take his money. But he didn't care about the money. It was his wife and two beautiful daughters, who were in their early twenties, that were at risk. Jones would gladly give his life to protect his family. He plotted what he would do when the car came to a stop.

He could wait until they got out of their car and then floor his and try to run a couple of them over and escape. But there was no way he could out run that car. What if these guys had guns? Most likely they did, because who would drive around at night stopping other cars unless they had a gun. Yeah, Jones was a hundred percent sure they had guns.

The cars were slowly rolling to a stop with the bad guys' car right on his front bumper. They had slowed down to 20 mph. Jones slammed on the brakes and pulled over to the side of the highway and stopped. The other car rolled to a stop about 50 feet in front of them.

Jones thought, *should I floor it and drive around them? No, they'd just pass us again. Should I do a U-turn and go back the way we came?*

Should I confront them? Should I just give up and let them have their way and beg them not to kill us? He didn't know what to do.

Jones said a prayer as the nightmare car started to back up. It moved to within ten feet of the Jones' front bumper. They could see the four men in the car very clearly.

They were trapped and afraid of what was about to happen. Mrs. Jones, screamed at her husband, "For God's sake, do something!"

WHAT WOULD YOU DO? (Read further to find out what Mr. Jones did ... it could save your life.)

COMMENTS

Here we go again with the Second Amendment debate. Who is right? Should we be able to own guns to hunt, collect, or use for self-defense? After all, it is our right to do so according to the United States Constitution. Or should the government be able to ban guns and outlaw any ownership? After all, that is the goal of the anti-gunners. There are thousands of gun laws on the books to control who can own one, where you can carry one, where you can own one, where you can shoot one, and what type of gun is illegal.

The truth is, none of those laws work because banning guns is like banning alcohol, which was attempted, but it didn't work too well. A large black market was started to sell booze. During that time period, crime and murders sky rocketed.

If you ban guns there will be a large black market to sell them. There are already black markets in every major city. Anyone can go out and buy an illegal gun from the shady neighborhood gun dealer. People living in that neighborhood know who those gun dealers are. But they don't report them because everyone in those poor neighborhoods want or need a gun to protect themselves.

STORY ONE CONTINUED
"THE KEY WEST TRIP"
What Would You Do?

Well, thank God that Mr. Jones and his family were avid gun owners. They would go shooting as a family every Thursday. They had carry permits and were armed with two 9mm Glocks that dark scary night.

Jones kept his headlights on the car, which was now directly in front of them. He advised his daughters to duck down behind the car seat. He told his wife, "If I get shot, you and the girls protect yourself. If I go down, shoot to kill. Don't let them get the girls."

Mr. and Mrs. Jones both racked a round into their Glock 17 pistols. He reminded his wife, "Keep your finger off the trigger, and don't shoot unless I tell you. Aim for their chests." They glanced at each other as he opened his car door. Mrs. Jones watched him and followed exactly what her husband did. Getting behind the driver's door, he aimed his gun at the car from hell. Jones shouted, "We are armed! If you step out of the car we will shoot!" After a few minutes there was no response from the men in the car. He repeated, "We are armed and will shoot if you step out of the car!"

His plan was to shoot the first person who

stepped out of the car. As soon as he could see a person's torso, he would fire two rounds at center mass. Shoot first and ask questions later. These guys weren't stopping them to ask for directions. Minutes ticked by and no one stepped out of the car. No one said a word. Jones was sweating in the hot steamy night. The stress was unbearable. He wondered if he should shout again. He kept his eyes open, carefully watching for a door to open, as he wiped the sweat from his brow.

After what seemed like an hour, the car suddenly revved its motor and sped away, while burning rubber, never to be seen again. The nightmare was over. They didn't have the guts to test if Jones really had a gun. What a relief it was to watch them pull away.

The Jones family sat there for a while speechless. It was like 2,000 pounds had just been lifted off of his shoulders. He breathed a sigh of relief, bowed his head, and said, "Thank you, God." Jones lit a smoke to calm his nerves. He noticed his hands were still shaking from the adrenaline. They sat there until another car passed them going in the same direction. Jones figured he'd follow that car just to be safe. Finally, Jones told his family, "It's safe now. Let's go home."

The odd thing was, the car from hell just disappeared into thin air. An hour later, Jones found a State Trooper in Naples, 50 miles away, and reported the incident. The trooper advised that these men had been robbing cars along the Interstate for a few weeks. He said that Jones was lucky to be armed. They would have taken his money and car, leaving them stranded in gator alley. Who knows what would have happened to his daughters.

Jones never heard from the police or found out what happen to those men. But that is typical because many crimes never get solved. The police are simply overwhelmed.

Being trained in the use of handguns, Jones knew what to do and would have done it to protect his family. But what if he didn't have a gun? What if you didn't have a gun?

WHAT WOULD YOU DO?

COMMENTS

The simple fact is the government or police can't control the sale of guns anymore than they can control the sale of dope on the streets. All the government can do is stop honest people, the law abiding people, from buying guns. The criminals, bad guys, and even terrorists all have access to guns. Guns can easily be smuggled over the borders. Our government doesn't fully protect the borders. We let almost anyone who can walk across the border into the United States. You can bet that many of them bring guns with them. The criminals bring in dope and guns for sure. The problem is, you never hear about that on the news.

One of my friends asked me if he should buy some gold for protection in case of a government or currency collapse. I told him no. I would buy guns and ammunition for protection as someone with guns can take all your gold and food. Guns and ammunition could be the currency with the most value if there is some kind of disaster. The most important item to own is a gun, and several guns are even better. In a survival state, man reverts to his basic instincts such as: self-protection, food, shelter, and water. It is desirable to own a gun to protect your family and friends if necessary. The Police cannot always be there for your protection. However, you need to learn how to use a gun in an efficient and safe manner.

STORY TWO
"SLEEP TIGHT,
YOU'RE SAFE AT HOME"

The Smith family lived in a middle-income neighborhood. They had lived in the same house for years. It was the same house that Mr. Smith grew up in from the age of ten. He knew that house inside-out and upside-down. It was a seventy- year-old three-story colonial home; the kind that had a dark dingy basement, and a musty smelling attic. Three bedrooms were located on the second floor. The house had a front door, side door, and rear door. The doors were big old thick wooden ones that had dead bolts and security chains on them. No one was going to break-in through those doors.

When he was a kid, Smith and his brothers pretended the house was a castle because large wooden steps wound all the way from the basement up to the attic. Often they played hide and seek, running up and down the steps. Each step on the old wooden stairway made a different creak or groan when stepped on. It got to the point where he could tell what step someone was on just by the type of creak it made.

The area they lived in was safe. As a matter of fact, it was very safc. No one, that he knew, had ever been robbed or had their car broken into. No one on his street, in all the years he lived there, ever had the slightest problem. The neighbors all knew each other and would report any strangers milling around to the police right away.

Mr. Smith had purchased this house from his parents after they moved to New York a few years ago. His Father gave him a good deal because Smith's wife was expecting a baby. It was their first baby, and it was the first grandchild in the family.

Smith had a security job working for a Department of Defense subcontractor. His wife hated that job because he had to carry a gun. He worked all kinds of hours, including being gone at night away on trips. But she felt safe and secure in their little home. Smith's wife hated guns so much that she made him keep his in the car trunk, locked in the garage. She always said, "I will not tolerate guns in the house." She wanted him to get another job. But the job put food on the table and it paid above average money in those days. So, Mr. Smith, being a good husband, followed his wife's wishes now that a baby was in the house. He knew the neighborhood was safe and didn't even give a second thought about keeping his gun in the trunk.

One night, the Smiths tucked in their baby and later they went to sleep early because Mr. Smith had a long drive the next day. They were sound asleep and safe in the old house. Or so they thought.

A slight unusual noise woke Smith up. He was a light sleeper and even a pin dropping on the floor would wake him. His wife, on the other hand, could sleep through a bomb explosion. He sat up in bed and cocked his ear toward the hallway. He heard something for sure. Some kind of noise came from downstairs. He sat there listening for several more minutes, but he didn't hear anything else so he tried to go back to sleep, thinking it must have been the cat.

He was almost asleep, but once again he heard another noise. It was a noise that he knew all too well. Someone was in the house. Someone was slowly walking across the old wooden floor leading to the steps, trying to be careful not to make any noise. But Smith knew that was impossible to do. Judging by the sounds, he determined that there was probably only one person. But he wasn't sure.

He shook his wife and put his hand over her mouth. Smith whispered in here ear, "Wake up, someone is in the house. Call the police from under the covers so they won't hear you." She followed his instructions.

Smith thought, *man I am screwed, what if this guy has a gun? What the hell will I do?* He got out of bed and quickly, but quietly, put on his pants and shoes. He listened for the intruder to determine where he was. Smith determined the person in the house was still on the first floor, possibly in the living room. He thought, *I only have one advantage over this intruder. I know this house and every squeak on the stairs. I need to take advantage of that.*

Mrs. Smith took the baby and hid under the bed as her husband had instructed. They were safe for now. Smith thought, *maybe I should yell out that I have a gun and the guy might leave. On second thought, no, bad idea. What if the intruder does have a gun?* He didn't want bullets being fired randomly into the bedrooms. So, he had no choice but to take him by surprise in hand-to-hand combat.

Smith hid at the top of the stairs, around the corner from the top step. He thought, *if only I had a gun or even a knife.* Then he remembered he did have a small pocket knife that he always carried. It was a knife that his father gave him years ago. He pulled it out and opened the blade. It was sharp because he kept it that way. He formulated a plan to jump the intruder and stab him in the heart, or even the throat, as soon as he detected him at the top of the stairs. That meant they would probably both fall down the flight of ten steps.

Smith ran the picture in his mind of what he was going to do. He visualized the blade plunging into the intruder's chest. He visualized them tumbling down the stairs with him on top, stabbing the guy.

Smith though, *if only I had my gun. Damn it*

anyhow, because of my wife's hatred for guns we could all be killed. If he has a gun, I'll try to take it away from him. If there are two of them I could be screwed. He tried not to think of that. One man he could handle, in most cases, but two was another story.

He could hear the man coming up the steps towards the second floor. He only heard one set of footsteps, which made him feel better. Ten more steps to the landing and then another ten to the top of the stairs. As he waited, Smith squeezed the handle of the knife.

Slowly the intruder inched up the stairs, one by one. Smith counted the steps and now the dirt bag was on the landing, just ten stairs away. The landing floor squeaked as the intruder moved across it. Every step squeaked or creaked with its own unique sound, so no matter how hard you tried not to make any noise, the steps would give you away.

Smith was ready and took deep breath. His adrenaline was pumping and his hands shook. Then he heard the creak he was waiting for and raised his knife. He knew it was the intruder or him that was going to die.

WHAT WOULD YOU DO? (Read further to find out what Mr. Smith did ... it may save your life.)

COMMENTS

The terrorists and criminals would love it if law abiding people could not purchase guns. If honest citizens had no weapons, other than a baseball bat, then the criminals would run rampant. The United States would turn into a third world country, like Iraq and Syria, as well as other countries around the world where the police are out-gunned and out-manned.

Our country would turn into a full blown Police State to control crime and weapons. Very simply, there are more bad guys than good guys once you take away the guns. The good guys are the police and law enforcement agencies, as well as honest freedom loving gun owners. Together they out-number the criminals. This is an important point. Take the guns away from honest freedom loving Americans and it won't be long before criminals/terrorists would out number and overwhelm the police. If you don't believe that, just look at Chicago, Detroit, East L.A., as well as our Capital. The police can't keep up with the criminal activities. Just ask them, they are overwhelmed.

Terrorists are very careful where they attack and it is always in a gun-free zone, where people are helpless. Take guns away from the people and the terrorists will have a free hand. Can we take that risk?

The fact is, if a government wants to control its citizens, then take away their power by disarming them. Hitler did it and so did many other dictators throughout history. You say that's impossible and won't happen here; our government wouldn't do that. No, they wouldn't do that right now. Tell that to the Germans, Italians, North Koreans, and Russian people from yesteryears. They didn't think the government would take their guns.

STORY TWO CONTINUED
"SLEEP TIGHT,
YOU'RE SAFE AT HOME"
What Would You Do?

Smith launched himself into the air giving a loud yell, while plunging his knife into the intruder's chest using his right hand. He grabbed the guy's left arm for support and held on to the knife as they tumbled down ten steps to the landing.

He landed on top of the criminal with his knife still stuck in the man's upper chest, right below the collar bone. His knife missed the guy's heart. The intruder was alive and fighting back. The man was strong and tried to remove the knife from his shoulder by grabbing Smith's right wrist. Smith leaned into the blade and twisted it, using both hands. The robber punched Smith in the face a couple of times, stunning him. Smith was dazed, but managed to pin the jerk's right arm using his knee. Smith thought, *this skinny jerk is super strong so he must be on speed or meth*. The knife didn't even seem to hurt him. It took all of Smith's strength to hold him down.

He thought about removing the blade and stabbing the intruder again, but the guy was just too strong. Smith feared once he pulled the knife out, the jerk might be able to take it from him. Smith was losing his strength quickly, but then a second burst of energy shot through him when he heard his wife yell.

Smith's wife, Joyce, came out of the bedroom, down to the landing, and screamed, "Kill him! Kill him!" Mr. Smith told his hysterical wife to shut-up and go let the cops inside, because they were banging on the door. The police came up to the landing and grabbed Smith by mistake, but his wife quickly corrected the officers.

They handcuffed the dirt bag and called an ambulance to the scene. As the police hauled the intruder away, he yelled, "I'll be back to get you! I'll get you for this!" The cop slapped him in the head and pushed him down the stairs.

Smith sat down on the steps, completely drained of energy. He couldn't stop his legs and hands from shaking. One police officer asked, "Are you ok?" Smith had blood all over his face and chest.

He looked up at him with his bloody bruised face and swollen eyes, and replied, "Yeah, I'm ok now." But Smith felt sick from the life and death struggle. He felt like he was going to vomit, but managed to hold it in.

A cop, named Kelly, who was a friend of Smith, said, "You could have killed that scumbag junkie and it would have been justified. I think this is the same guy we've been looking for. You sure are lucky. He had a gun on him."

Smith didn't reply, but thought, *Kelly was right, I should have killed him since the junkie threatened to come back.* Then it occurred to him this wasn't over yet because there would be a trial. They would have to testify in court.

It went to trial and the intruder received four years jail time and six years probation. At the trial, the junkie starred at Smith with evil eyes the entire time. Then Smith's wife remembered what the junkie had said. She was very concerned that he'd come back to get them when he was released from prison.

The good thing that came out of this was Mrs. Smith became pro-gun. She learned to shoot and protect herself. Now their house has guns stored in safe, yet handy places. Now they can sleep at night without so much fear. But in the back of their minds they worry every night about the junkie coming back.

Two years later, the junkie was released from jail. The police called Smith to warn him the criminal was being released early. How could anyone only receive two years for armed robbery? Oh, it wasn't armed robbery because he never took anything. It was only assault and attempted robbery, along with a breaking and entering charge. What about an attempted murder charge? That was thrown out because there was no proof that he wanted to kill Mr. Smith. What about the gun he had? It became lost evidence, so they couldn't prove he had a gun.

What about the traumatic experience the Smith family went through? The Smiths were violated in their own home. After a break-in you never feel safe again in your home. Justice doesn't care about that. Justice is blind and the victims do suffer.

The junkie hasn't returned to the Smith's house, but if he does it will be a different story next time. Mrs. Smith is waiting for him. She is waiting to give him past due justice for putting her through hell.

Sleep tight, you're safe at home.

WHAT WOULD YOU DO?

COMMENTS

Taking away guns or banning guns will not keep America safer. Case in point, look at Chicago. It has one of the highest murder rates in the United States and some of the toughest gun laws. Where do these criminals obtain their guns? They buy them from the black market, of course. No background check is needed, only cold hard cash. No questions are asked. No gun registration is required. They laugh at the gun laws.

There is a big black market for guns in Chicago because the gun laws have made it that way. Criminals always want what is illegal or banned by the government. Why is this? One word … MONEY. They can make big money selling those illegal weapons.

STORY THREE
"LET'S GO TO THE MOVIES"

Everyone goes to the movies once in a while. Mr. and Mrs. Hill go every Friday because it's one of their retirement hobbies. Every Friday, new movies come out so they pick one and spend the afternoon enjoying a movie, popcorn, and a Coke. Usually, before the movies, they go to one of their favorite restaurants and have lunch. Then they walk to the theater just down the street a few blocks away.

They live in a fairly large city of over 1 million people. It has a very safe downtown area where the theater is located. Police do their normal patrols and are watchful of people acting strangely. The theater is located in a public square setting with people always walking around or milling about shopping.

The Hills park their car in the local five story parking garage next door to the theater because parking is free if you save your ticket stub. It's a short ten minute walk between the two locations.

The Hills have done this movie routine every Friday for fifteen years. They have never had any problems. However, they are aware that sometimes crimes are commented in the vicinity, but mostly at the night, so they always go to the movies in the afternoon.

As they walked up to the theater, they noticed there was already a line of fifteen people ahead of them. It was the new Superman movie and the crowds would be big. They got into line and a short time later a man got in line behind them.

Mr. Hill is an alert person and he moved his wife in front of him when he saw the big dude who got in line behind her. Hill knew that there were people who would snatch your purse and run. Hill didn't like the way this man looked. He was big, towering over Hill, at about six four or five, and had a shabby appearance to him.

As the line moved forward, he could feel this big guy bumping into him, brushing up against Hill's backside. Hill had his wallet in his front pocket like he always did, aware that there were pickpockets. This type of action was indicative of a pickpocket, Hill thought.

After several times of being bumped by this man, Hill turned around and advised him to keep his distance. The man didn't say a word back to Hill. By now there were thirty people in line behind them. The line inched forward and the Hills reached the ticket window, which was located outside of the theater. Hill's wife went to pay for the tickets and the big jerk bumped into Hill again and was leaning over Hill's shoulder, looking at their money on the ticket counter.

Hill turned around and said, "I told you to stay

back and not touch me!"

The big jerk was right in Hill's face and said, "Screw you." Then he gave Mr. Hill a hard shove backwards into Mrs. Hill, which pushed her, making her drop the money and purse.

With that confrontation, and without any hesitation, Hill turned and punched him hard as he could in the sternum. It knocked the wind out of the man and he fell on his back to the pavement. Women started screaming as Hill stepped on the man's throat. Hill told him, "Don't get up, or I'll hurt you."

Mr. Hill is no spring chicken, being 63 years old, but he's in pretty good shape for his age. His years spent in the military made him fearless.

No one in line stepped up to help old man Hill. One person actually told Hill to leave the poor man alone. Hill didn't reply to the stupid person and kept his foot on the jerk's throat until he almost passed out. No one asked what happened or offered any help.

The only person who really knew what had happened was the young man who was the ticket agent. He told Hill, "Nice moves, Mister," as he slid the tickets under the window. Hill watched as his wife picked up their money off the ground.

The jerk laid there, gasping for breath, as the Hills went into the movies. Needless to say, Hill's adrenaline was really pumping. He didn't feel like going to the movies now.

As they walked into the theater, Hill's wife asked, "What's wrong with that guy?"

Mr. Hill simply said, "He's a crook looking to steal something from an easy mark."

"Maybe you should have called the police," she said.

"He didn't break any laws and besides, I hit him first, so I'd probably go to jail."

Waiting in line for their popcorn, Hill saw the trouble-maker come in the theater and stand back by the game machines. The Hills went to get their seat and the man followed them. Mr. Hill picked a seat near the door, on the end of a row.

A minute later, the jerk walked in past them. They exchanged glances. Mr. Hill watched the man pick a seat behind them but on the other side of the theater. The movie started but Hill couldn't sit there knowing this weirdo was behind him.

After half an hour, Mr. Hill told his wife, "Let's leave. I can't enjoy the movie with that guy here." So they left and went for a coffee next door. Upon leaving the coffee shop, Hill spotted the same man walking towards the parking garage. That was where they were going next. Hill took his time and didn't want to worry his wife, so he didn't tell her that he saw the jerk.

Making it back to the garage, their car was on the second floor. Hill had his radar on looking for the big dude but didn't see him. As they approached their car, a man got out of the vehicle next to it. To Hill's surprise it was the crook. He blocked their way to the car.

"Give me your wallet and purse," the crook said.

Hill heard footsteps behind him. Thinking someone would help them, he turned to look. There was another man, but he wasn't there to help them. "Yeah, hand it over now and you won't get hurt, old man," he said, with an evil grin on his face.

The big jerk said, "I owe you a punch or two, so hurry it up, before I beat the crap out of you."

WHAT WOULD YOU DO? (Read further to find out what Mr. Hill did … it may save your life.)

COMMENTS

Then there are the elites, the rich and famous, or maybe not famous, but rich. They live in the gated communities, away from crime areas. They have their armed security and you can bet most of them own guns. But it's ok for them because they are rich. They can do what they want to. They don't have to live with the common people, associate with the common people, or even go to the same shopping malls that common people do.

Finally, there are the elected officials. Most mayors of big cities have police security with them 24-7. They have a security detail assigned to cover them even after they are out of office. Congressional representatives and senators all have some type of security. They live and work in secure places and don't really have to worry about crime or terrorists. You can bet they all own some type of weapon. If the elites and those in power can protect themselves, why can't average honest Americans have the right to protect themselves?

STORY THREE CONTINUED
"LET'S GO TO THE MOVIES"
What Would You Do?

Mr. Hill closely observed the two men who stood in front of him. Neither one showed that they had a gun, but the big jerk did have one hand in his pocket, which indicated that he might have a weapon of some type. They didn't look that tough, and Hill had already knocked the big guy to the ground earlier.

Mrs. Hill clinched her purse. She didn't want these guys to take their Social Security money. They were on a tight budget. If they took this money it would financially hurt them for a while.

Mr. Hill didn't expect this; it totally caught him off guard. His brain was racing. What should he do? Should he take these two crooks on or let them have their way? Hill didn't want to endanger his wife and that was his main concern.

"Come on, old man! Hurry it up or we'll hurt you both," the jerk said.

Hill knew his skill. He was old but had a lot of experience under his belt. He knew what he could do and couldn't do. Yeah, if he was just ten years younger and didn't have a bad shoulder, he could probably whip both men, at the same time. He had training that was ingrained into his muscle reflexes.

But what if these men do have guns? If so, why don't they show them? Why don't they point their guns at him and force him to hand over their money. The more those thoughts raced through his brain, the more he sensed that these muggers did not have a gun.

Hill said, "I'll give you our money but not our wallets." He wanted to see what they would say.

"We want your credit cards, too. Hand it over now! I'm getting pissed off," the big jerk replied.

"Ok, ok. Honey, give them your purse."

His wife shouted, "I will not!"

Both men looked at her and one stepped forward to take it out of her hands. He grabbed it, but she wouldn't let go. Both men were distracted by the commotion. The guy knocked Mrs. Hill to the ground and took her purse. He had just made a big mistake, because this really made old man Hill angry.

Hill made his move as their eyes were fixed on his wife and the purse. He quickly pulled out his pocket gun, a Ruger LCP 380 pistol. In one swift motion, he cocked it and flicked off the safety. As he pointed the gun at the men they were shocked, to say the least. Hill said, "Put your hands in the air and get on your knees. I'm not afraid to shoot if I have to."

The big jerk said, "Come on mister, we weren't gonna hurt you guys."

Hill replied, "Shut up! Don't move or I will shoot … and I never miss."

Hill helped his wife get up from the floor and told her to call the police. While waiting for the cops, some other people came along and helped Hill keep any eye on the crooks until the police arrived.

Mr. Hill always carried a little pocket gun ever since he received his weapons permit years ago. He never had to pull his gun out until now. Actually, his wife told him he was overreacting always carrying a gun to the movies or to the shopping mall.

Mr. and Mrs. Hill went to the trial to testify against the criminals. The judge threw the book at them because this was their third offense. One received six years and the big jerk got eight years. Oh, by the way, they didn't have any guns but they did have oversized knives. Knives with blades longer than four inches are considered concealed weapons according to the state law. You need a concealed weapons permit to carry one, which they didn't have.

Apparently, the men were already parked in the garage when the Hills pulled in next to them. The Hills unknowingly became their target that day. Yes, the big jerk did try to pick his pocket in line at the theater.

The Hills still go to the movies every Friday, but are more careful where they park. If someone is just sitting in a car nearby, they park in another place.

What would have happened if Mr. Hill didn't have a gun? What if you didn't have a gun?

WHAT WOULD YOU DO?

COMMENTS

Now, if you are new to guns, a life-long NRA member, or an anti-gunner, I hope the following makes sense to you. Anti-gunners should be thankful that there are still honest law abiding people who carry guns or have them at home. These honest Americans indirectly help keep crime rates down. They indirectly help keep the terrorists at bay. With millions of Americans owning guns, it is virtually impossible for a terrorist group like ISIS to take over a city or the country.

STORY FOUR
"KNOCK, KNOCK, GUESS WHO'S THERE?"

Mr. and Mrs. Dole live on a quiet street in a virtually crime free upper-class neighborhood. They have lived here many years and never had one problem with criminals or misfits in the area. The neighborhood association has hired armed police around the clock. People who live here have money and are very well-off.

The Doles have a lovely dream home, which they take great pride in. It's a fairly modern home with two bedrooms on the first floor, one of which is the master bedroom and another bedroom upstairs, which is used for an office.

Everyone pretty much knows everyone else in this little community, which has a population of about 3,000 people. Many people go to the only local bar, which is open until 3 am, for a drink after work or for a nightcap. Everyone knows each other and it is a friendly enjoyable atmosphere. Bartenders who have worked there for years know all the usual customers, so when a stranger stops in this off-the-beaten-path bar, they take notice.

Tim Dole is in his mid-forties and his wife, Sue, is much younger at the ripe old age of twenty-five. The Doles are social people. They always go out to eat and drink at establishments all around town. They were invited to all the big parties, and also had a few parties themselves.

Sue is Tim's eye candy. She's a trophy wife and Tim takes pride in the fact that his wife is a real knockout, a definite ten. Everyone knows them in the area and they are known for drinking too much, often until late in the morning.

One Saturday night, the Doles were at the local bar drinking until 1 am in the morning. The bartenders had to ask them to leave because Tim was beyond drunk. His wife had to drive them home.

The story goes that Tim had a few more drinks and passed out at home on the couch. Sue, his wife, was still awake and watching TV with her little dog. The toy Poodle let out a low growl even before the knock on the door came. Someone coming to the door at two or three in the morning wasn't that unusual for the Doles. Neighbors would sometimes drop in for a night cap to swap rumors or discuss the day's news, if they saw the lights on.

Sue got up, holding her little dog in her arms and went to answer the door. Their front door did not have a peek hole to check who was there. Sue was too trustworthy, being a girl from a small city in the Midwest. She didn't think anything of opening the door in the middle of the night without knowing who was there. She had a laissez-faire attitude about her. That's just the way she acted. It seemed that nothing fazed her.

The knock came again, only louder. Sue yelled, as she approached the door, "Come on in, it's unlocked!"

The door swung open, and to her great shock a man wearing a mask burst inside and ran towards her at full speed. He grabbed her and knocked the little dog to the ground. He put his arms around her, while holding her from behind, and covered her mouth so she couldn't scream. It happened in a split second and she couldn't fight off the big brut, he was just too strong.

She started kicking her feet and he held her up in the air. He whispered in her ear, "Give me your money. Don't fight me or I'll hurt you bad."

In the other room, Tim, her husband, was out on the couch. He was of no help. She nodded her head, indicating compliance to his orders. He removed his hand from her mouth so she could speak. When he did that she let out a scream, as loud as she could, and he bashed her in the head as she kept screaming.

Finally, Tim woke up. Hearing the screams, he drunkenly walked out of the living room into the foyer and was dumbfounded at what he saw. Tim sobered up right away and yelled, "What the hell are you doing?" Tim jumped on the man, who then released Sue.

The two exchanged blows but the intruder got the best of Tim and knocked him to the floor, dazing him. Then the masked man jumped on top of him, straddling his chest, and began to ground and pound Tim's face. The whole time he was yelling over and over, "Give me your money!"

Sue, in an effort to save her husband, jumped on the intruders back but he grabbed her by the hair and threw her across the room. She came back and attempted to help her husband again, but the guy backhanded her in the face. Her nose was bleeding and she was shook-up.

Getting up, Sue observed that Tim was almost knocked out, and was basically getting pummeled to death. He wasn't even trying to fight back, or block the punches from the raving maniac. She ran into the master bedroom and locked the door.

WHAT WOULD YOU DO? (Read further and find out what Sue Dole did ... it may save your life.)

COMMENTS

The problem is, you won't read in the newspapers or hear on the news how everyday men and women stop a robbery or murder using their gun. Almost every day, a law abiding citizen is putting his life on the line to stop a criminal act. The police can't be everywhere. It takes minutes for the police to respond. By that time the crime is done. Unless you have your own bodyguard by your side, you will be in trouble.

If you don't want to own a gun, fine, but don't try to stop those law abiding citizens who want a gun for hunting, a hobby, or protection from having one. Your life may depend on one of these armed citizens one day.

STORY FOUR CONTINUED
"KNOCK, KNOCK,
GUESS WHO'S THERE?"
What Would You Do?

Sue ran into her bedroom and locked the door. She thought, *should I call 911? No, by the time they get here this guy will have killed Tim and then he'd start on me.* There was only one solution.

It so happens that this man, this intruder, did not randomly pick the Dole's house to rob. He had been scoping the Doles out all night while he sat in the corner of the bar, sipping on a beer. He saw Tim flashing around his money acting like a rich fool. He saw Tim's big wad of cash that he laid on the bar counter every now and then. He needed money badly, and the more he observed Tim the more he wanted to take his money. He also thought Tim's hot wife would be a bonus, and wanted her also. If he could just spend a few minutes with her, he'd let her know what a real man was like.

No one knew that this man had just got out of prison a few weeks ago after serving ten years for assault and robbery. His modus operandi was not to use a gun or weapon, because if he was caught with one the jail time would be a lot longer. So, he used his fists as weapons. The last man he assaulted had his brain turned to mush and suffered from irreversible brain damage.

Yes, this big dude was a bad ass. Built like a fullback with a thick neck, hard head, and muscular body. He was a fighter that rarely lost a battle. Muscles popped out of his arms from ten years of lifting weights in prison. Those muscles needed to be exercised. He needed to let out his stress on someone, and he needed money. Tim was the perfect target.

It was discovered that the dirt bag came to Florida, from up north, because his friends had moved here while he was in prison. They told him Florida was easy pickins because of the old people and rich socialites living there.

Sue stood there for a second, opened her dresser drawer, and pulled out her new Lady Smith & Wesson .38 special revolver, model 642LS. She had just purchased this gun, two months ago, when she received her concealed weapons permit. Her hands shook as she picked up the bullets, one by one, and slid them into the chamber. After putting in five rounds she thought to herself, *come on Sue, you can do this.* Sue had only fired this gun three or four times at the range. She wasn't a good shot and feared she might hit her husband.

With gun in hand, she rushed back into the foyer. Tim was a bloody mess and the robber was still yelling, "Where is the money?" The intruder glanced at her holding the gun, but he didn't stop punching Tim's face. Being extremely careful, she took aim at him.

The first round she fired didn't seem to do anything to him. She wondered if she even hit him. He kept bashing Tim's face, while he looked at her, and said, "Tell me where the money is or I'm gonna kill him."

Sue moved around behind him and carefully took aim. She fired another round and another one into the intruder. Finally, he stood up, waived his hands, and said, "No, more. Give me that gun," as he stumbled towards her to grab the gun.

Sue fired one more time. It was the kill shot. It took four rounds to stop this big monster. He fell to the tile floor, in front of her, and didn't move.

Sue called 911, and soon the police and an ambulance were at the scene. After an investigation, it was ruled a justified shooting of a home invader. Tim was beat up pretty good, broken nose and fractured jaw, but no brain damage that they could tell. But detecting brain damage from blows to the head sometimes takes years to discover.

The whole incident took a toll on both of them. They made one mistake and did not seek professional medical help for mental stress or PTSD. After this incident, Tim and Sue carried a gun everywhere they went. They became paranoid that people were out to get them. A year later, sadly, they were divorced.

The Doles were very lucky that Sue had a gun and knew how to use it. But what if she didn't have a gun? What if you didn't have a gun? Next time when someone knocks on your door, think about it.

WHAT WOULD YOU DO?

COMMENTS

The previous four stories were based on real events that did transpire. The names were changed to protect the innocent, and the stories were fictionalized somewhat to add suspense and realism.

Most incidents like these happen in a matter of minutes or seconds. They happen when you least expect them. These events always seem to happen when the police are not around.

What would you do? What will you do? Use common sense and protect yourself.

PART TWO

THE SECOND AMENDMENT, COMMENTS, AND THOUGHTS

The right to bear arms goes back to the beginning of mankind. For example, if you just observe history, every culture had weapons. The American Indians and Africans had spears and bows, as well as knives. These weapons were around for thousands of years, along with the sword. Some Kings tried to ban weapons, which didn't work out too well. In Europe, the Knights were supposed to be the only ones who could carry a sword. In Japan, it was the Samurai who could only carry swords. To learn swordsmanship took skillful training and strength. It was up close in-your-face combat. Learning to use a bow and arrow or spear was a lot easier. In addition, using a bow didn't require great strength and it was not used as a close quarter combat weapon. Using a sword requires a special breed of man for hand-to-hand combat, face-to-face fighting. The warrior had to have the skill, guts, strength, and willingness to kill, or be killed.

Then, the gun came along and actually made all men equal in combat, more or less. The gun is one of the top ten inventions of all time. It reduced hunger by improving man's hunting ability. A man could now defend his family or friends from their enemies or dangerous animals. Hence, everyone from the old world wanted to own a gun. It became a right to own one, just like the sword or bow. This right has carried forward to modern days.

As I mentioned earlier, the Second Amendment is a lot more than words. It is a type of thinking. It is a rational judgment made by free men that started long ago, before this country was founded. It came into full meaning at the battles of Concord and Lexington. First, let us examine the words and intention of the Second Amendment.

The 2ND Amendment: *"A well regulated Militia, being necessary to the security of a free State, the right of the people to keep and bear Arms, shall not be infringed."*

The beauty of the United States Constitution is that it was written so that normally educated men could understand the meaning, especially the Bill of Rights, which are the first Ten Amendments. These first Ten Amendments are interlinked and are the base of the Constitution. These are the backbone of the Constitution, which insure that the citizens can enjoy God Given Freedoms. The Constitution is the highest Law of the Land. Many people don't realize that point. The Constitution takes precedence over all other laws, be they state, city, or county.

In debating the meaning of the Second Amendment, attorneys and scholars become hung up on the definition of the words like, regulated Militia, State, and believe it or not, the right of the people to keep and bear arms.

When the United States was founded, the first battles for freedom were at Lexington and Concord, Massachusetts. At Concord it was called "The shot heard around the world." Who were these men? Who were these American Patriots that challenged the King of England and his laws? Who were these heroes that dared to take on the most powerful army in the world at the time?

They were nobody and everybody, from the farms and small towns of America. They were the everyday people, farmers, shop keepers, blacksmiths, ministers, and so forth. They made up the militia in each Colony. They had their own arms or weapons for hunting and self-defense.

One has to remember, that for one hundred years, the colonists had been fighting the Indians and the French. They already had experience fighting in groups for their survival in the new world. They already had formed a type of militia to protect their settlements. They were already organized as a well-regulated militia on their own without a central government. Each Colony and each town had their own volunteer forces made up of common people who would heed the call to battle when required to do so.

Depending where you look, the definition of militia has many different meanings. The best ones that I have found are: a military force that is raised from the civil population to supplement a regular

THOMAS H. WARD

army in an emergency; or a military force that engages in rebel or terrorist activities, typically in opposition to a regular army.

These definitions were taken from online searches. In no case does it mean that a Federal Army is the militia. The militia, at the time, had no central government. So this dispels the notion that militia means the same as an army controlled by a central government. Later, under the command of George Washington, the militia would be transformed into the first American Army.

The Battles of Lexington and Concord were the first major military engagements between the local settlers, or the so called Massachusetts Militia, and the Kingdom of Great Britain on April 19, 1775. The militia was made up of local settlers from the Lexington and Concord vicinity. This is where the first shots were fired. Why did this happen?

For many years, King George and his Army committed outrageous acts against the 13 Colonies and the people. They are too numerous to mention here, but all you have to do is read the Constitution to find out what some the outrageous acts were. Our wonderful Constitution limits the power of the government based on many of those unfair laws established by the British at the time.

The Massachusetts Colony responded to new strict laws from the King by forming an illegal patriot group, known as the Massachusetts Provincial Congress. It called for local militias to start training for possible war. Then, early in 1775 the King declared that the Colony of Massachusetts was in a state of rebellion.

Seven hundred British Regulars left Boston under orders to capture and destroy rebel military supplies, which consisted mainly of guns, gun powder, and lead balls. They were ordered to collect guns from the population outside of Boston, leaving them defenseless.

This was the straw the broke the camel's back. The Americans were never going to give up their weapons. The first shots were fired at sunrise in Lexington. Blood was spilled and tempers flared. The militia was outnumbered, so they fell back and regrouped. Later that day, at the North Bridge in Concord, four hundred American Militiamen stopped the King's troops and engaged them. To the surprise of the British troops and the militiamen, shots were again fired. This resulted in casualties on both sides, and forced the British Troops to withdraw back to Boston, their stronghold.

The militiamen chased them all the way back to Boston, while taking sniper shots along the way. Their blood ran hot as the Americans wanted to make a point. The point was don't try to take our guns and freedom. You could say they were our first Freedom Fighters.

Hence, the war was started. The first bullets

flew and the first blood was spilled to keep the British from taking American guns. **Make no mistake, this is the main reason we have the Second Amendment. It will insure that no tyrants could ever again subjugate American Citizens.**

Of course, there were many outrageous acts that actually caused the war, but it was the threat to take away the guns from the American Colonists that sparked the Revolution. If it wasn't for the brave Militiamen who engaged the Red Coats on that hot April day in 1775, who knows where we would be now?

So, as you can see, there is no big mystery of the meaning or definition of the Second Amendment. Complicated definitions are not necessary to explain the Second Amendment.

PART THREE

WHO SHOULD OWN GUNS?

Do we need gun laws? Yes, but we already have thousands of them. More laws will not do anything to stop the bad guys. Laws are only obeyed by the good citizens. Criminals and terrorist don't care about laws. Is that so hard to understand?

Should everyone be able own a gun? No, not everyone, that goes without saying. Mentally ill people, who have a history of committing violence, should not have access to a gun. Of course, felons and criminals should not have the ability to purchase a gun. Terrorists should never have the ability to own a gun. But how do you control this when illegal guns can be readily purchased? It cannot be totally controlled and more laws will not solve this problem. Enforcement of current laws would greatly help.

Building a database for background checks that includes: violent mentally ill people, the secret terrorist watch list, the secret no-fly list, and a violent ex-felon list would certainly help. The question is, who should control this list? The database must to be shared with state and local law enforcement departments. Currently there is not just one list, so this is a big loophole that needs to be closed.

It is possible that someone could be placed on one of these lists by mistake. Once you get on a list you don't even know it and it is almost impossible to get off of a list. In that case, you must have **due process to challenge the government, without cost to you, to be removed from that list** by going before a Federal Judge. Currently it is almost impossible to be removed from any government list.

Here's a question for you. After being interviewed by the FBI three times, why wasn't the Orlando shooter put on a list? Oh, it violated his rights, because he was not guilty of anything. At least that's what the FBI claims. The solution is simple. If someone is interviewed three times, then he is a suspicious character. He should be ban from purchasing guns for a period of time, until further surveillance is done. One year, three years, or five years, I don't know what amount of time would be appropriate, but it would depend upon what was found in further investigations. This is only common sense.

Another solution is, when someone goes to purchase a gun, state law enforcement is notified to conduct a background check on the spot. You are tracked by your name and SS number so your records can be reviewed, not only by the state, but by the FBI when your name is submitted for approval to purchase a gun. Of course, the only people in the data base should be criminals and known or aspiring terrorists. If such a database was actually being used and checked, it could possibly stop some of the terrorists. State Law Enforcement would be able to see that someone was interviewed three times by the FBI, and he wants to purchase a gun. Wouldn't that send up red flags? Ban that person from purchasing a gun for a time period to be determined. If you have been interviewed three times by the FBI, then you are a problem. Don't you think so? Isn't that common sense?

Yes, this is all well and good hindsight thinking. But what if the terrorist buys the guns on the black market or from a friend? This is what the San Bernardino terrorists did. Then there is no way to know about that purchase. What do we do about that? That is one of the problems. Maybe we can solve that problem. Please read further.

Should some types of guns be banned? No, because it's not the type of gun that kills, it's the type of person. Machine guns are already banned and have been for a long time. There is a push to ban so called assault weapons, which are defined as those guns that can hold multiple rounds, and look dangerous with a pistol grip. The terrorist could have used any type of gun to do what was done in Orlando. Any type of semi-automatic pistol would have done the same thing. A lever action Winchester rifle could have been used.

Anti-gunners usually come back with this: "The Second Amendment doesn't say what type of guns people may own. In those days, people only had single shot weapons. They didn't know we would have the types of guns we do today."

Right, the Second Amendment doesn't say what type of arms a person can or cannot own. It just says Arms. Yes, they had one shot muskets in the old days, but if they had AR 15s they would have used them at Concord. The Militia would be very pleased to have the type of weapons we have now. Most would agree that the type of weapons used would not have changed the wording of the Second Amendment.

PART FOUR

TERRORIST ATTACKS

> **AUTHOR'S NOTE:** *In writing about the terrorist attacks, I found it very depressing, and for lack of a better words, a dark place to go. Pure evil is associated with the events. Therefore, I did not mention the terrorists' names in this book.*

Has the government dropped the ball in protecting the home front? Yes, they have, because almost every time there is a mass terrorist attack, it turns out that some law enforcement agency had known that person was potentially dangerous. Let us examine the major terrorist attacks from recent years.

THE ORLANDO TERRORIST ATTACK

The June 2016 radical Islamist terrorist attack in Orlando was a terrible deed committed by a person born here, but of Muslim Afghan parents who immigrated here. No one really knows what influence his father had on him, but in Muslim families the father is the head of the household, and the most important figure.

The Orlando terrorist was **investigated three times by the FBI** between 2013 and 2014, after he was reported to them by the county Sheriff for making statements to his co-workers about **his**

connections with al-Qaida and claimed to be a member of Hezbollah. He was actually linked to a known terrorist who died committing a suicide bombing overseas. The perpetrator had made at least two **trips to Saudi Arabia** in 2011 and 2012.

He did go out and buy the guns legally that were used in the attack. Why wasn't he put on a no-buy list after being interviewed three times by the FBI? The weapons were used in a gun-free zone, because in Florida guns are not permitted in a bar/club situation were alcohol is served. How did this killer manage to carry an AR 15 rifle into the nightclub? Reports say that there was an off duty police officer at the door who engaged him. Whatever happened during that engagement? We'll never know for sure, but it is clear the door security, which is there to check IDs, did not stop the killer. A lot of people dropped the ball, including the FBI. **So how did he manage to get inside with a rifle?**

It seems that his wife had some knowledge of what was going on. Media reports, citing anonymous officials, state that his wife went with him to scout for possible targets and to purchase the ammunition. Was she involved? I think so, don't you?

SAN BERNADINO ATTACK

This attack was committed by a radical Muslim couple. He was an American born U.S. citizen of

Pakistani descent. His wife, a Pakistani, had moved apparently to Saudi Arabia before coming here. That alone is very suspicious because for a single woman to move to Saudi Arabia is impossible for most women, or men, to do. She had to have some type of mentor or sponsor there.

She was here legally on a visa and was issued a green card. **When you are issued a visa and green card, it is mandatory to conduct a background check.** They made trips back and forth to **Saudi Arabia in the years** prior to the attack. It is unclear how many trips were made. Law enforcement believes his wife was radicalized before moving to the United States, yet they still let her in the country on a visa.

The terrorists obtained their guns from the man living next door, who was married to the terrorist's older brother's wife's sister. This man is a United States citizen who converted to Islam, and became radicalized by the attackers. He purchased the guns legally and just gave them to the terrorists, apparently knowing what they were going to do.

The male terrorist worked for the California Department of Public Health. The couple attended the annual Christmas party, but not to celebrate Christmas. Somehow they managed to **sneak in their rifles,** along with few bombs into this soft target gun-free zone.

How did they manage to do this without

anyone seeing the weapons? It's amazing that no one saw them. They covered their faces, giving the impression that they fully expected to get away with killing a group of people.

The government says they were self-radicalized shooters or homegrown violent extremists. They forgot the words **Radical Islamic Terrorists.**

FORT HOOD ATTACK

In 2009, an Army Major fatally shot thirteen people and injured more than thirty at Fort Hood in Texas. He was a psychiatrist and a Muslim. He was not married and did not have many friends; he was a loner, so to speak. Where did he obtain his guns? He purchased them at a gun store even after he was known to be a possible threat.

Days after the shooting, it was discovered that he had been in communications, via email, with Yemen based Anwar al-Awlaki who was being monitored by the NSA, and was a known terrorist. **The NSA and the FBI knew that the Fort Hood shooter was becoming increasing more radical over the years.**

From 2003 to 2009 he was based at Walter Reed Medical Center for his internship. His supervisors, fellow students, and faculty were troubled by his behavior, which was described as paranoid, belligerent, and schizoid.

While presenting a paper at Walter Reed

Medical Hospital, he preached about Islam. He said, "According to the Koran, non-believers would be sent to hell, decapitated, set on fire, and have burning oil poured down their throats." This shocked his Army instructors. **But still, no red flags went up.**

This terrorist had over twenty email communications with Anwar al-Awlaki, a known terrorist. **The NSA knew this fact.** The FBI started to investigate the Fort Hood killer. What happened to that investigation? **Why was this nut case not arrested by the FBI or the military before the Fort Hood murders? Why wasn't his name placed on a no-buy gun list?**

Let's go back and look at one more terrorist attack. Let's look at the Boston Marathon Bombing in 2013. If they can't obtain guns, they will use bombs or anything else.

BOSTON MARATHON BOMBING

Two brothers committed this terrorist act. They were both devout Muslims, according to their aunt. **The FBI was informed by the Russian Federal Security Service in 2011 that they were radical Islamists. The FBI interviewed the whole family but did not find any evidence of terrorism activity.**

The older brother and mastermind of the attack made **trips back to his home** country. The older brother was also previously connected to a triple murder in Waltham, Massachusetts in 2011, but nothing came of that connection because of the lack of evidence.

Some analysts claim the brothers' mother was a radical extremist and supporter of Jihad. It was thought that she influenced her sons' behavior. **The Russian government warned the United States two times about the family.**

The older brother and his mother were put on the terrorism watch list about a year and a half before the bombing took place. Were they being watched by the FBI at the time? No one knows what the FBI was doing. What do they do when you are placed on the terrorism watch list? **Do they watch you?**

The younger brother said his older brother wanted to defend Islam from the United States for starting wars in the Middle-East Muslim countries. He said the bombings were retribution for the United States military killing thousands of innocent Muslims.

Who dropped the ball here?

ANALYSIS

Those were the basic short summaries about four terrorist incidents from the recent past. Now, let's look at what they all had in common. First, all the terrorists were **radical** Muslims. Second, all were **investigated by the FBI** with the exception of the San Bernardino shooters. Third, they all had contacts with other radical Islamic persons, and in two cases they took trips to Saudi Arabia. They all read radical information from the internet and communicated with people by email. Fourth, they all somehow managed to **smuggle guns or bombs into a gun-free zone.** Three of the four had **government jobs** of some type.

For the San Bernardino terrorist, however, the government knew the background of his imported wife. She came here on a visa, and should have had a background check. We do not know if she was given one or not. The FBI, or some government agency, knew they had made trips to Saudi Arabia, which is where nine of the eleven hijackers came from that took down the World Trade Center towers. Anyone from Saudi Arabia should have raised a red flag.

Did it strike you weird that in three of these cases terrorists were investigated by the FBI? What the hell is going on? Was the ball dropped and these terrorists slipped through the cracks of justice? It appears so to this writer. What do we do about this? Maybe the FBI procedures need to be changed.

Is the FBI infiltrated with radical Muslims who try to cover up for those about to commit terrorist acts? I don't know, I am just throwing that scary thought out there. Or maybe the PC police just overlooked them because they were Muslim. That is Political Correctness gone way too far. PC has no business in the FBI.

SUMMARY of TERRORISTS ATTACKS

Look at the all the items in common with each terrorist attack. The fact that the FBI knew about these people in three of the four cases is the number one thing that sticks out in my mind. They were all radical Muslims. In the bombing case, the FBI was even warned the about these people by the Russians, far ahead of time. For the most part, it appears those warnings went unheeded. Why?

The other thing that strikes me is how they all got past security with guns or a bomb. People really need to pay closer attention as to what is going on around them.

Are people dropping the ball because of political correctness? Or is our national security really that inept. I would like to think that political correctness is to blame. Does the FBI need to be investigated for letting political correctness stand in the way?

PART FIVE

CONCLUSIONS, SOLUTIONS, and FINAL REMARKS

How are we going to solve these problems? How are we going to stop the terrorists, whom I fear will start using more bombs in the future? I'd rather face a man with a gun than with a bomb.

There are some solutions on how to stop these terrorists, and it's not by making more gun laws. Everyone knows it will take profiling. I don't see anything wrong with that. If you haven't done anything wrong and you're not going to commit a terrorist act, then you have nothing to fear.

When we board an airplane, we're all presumed guilty of being a terrorist because they check our bodies and luggage. That isn't right, but it is the law. After 911 the terrorists were able to take away some of our freedom. Do you want any more taken?

We are at war, and during the Second World War we profiled Germans, Italians, and Japanese because at the time those governments were our enemies. It didn't matter that many of the people profiled were American-born citizens. Was it the right thing to do at the time? I don't know, but it worked.

Radical Islamic terrorists are everyone's enemies. They will kill other Muslims, Christians, Jews, non-believers, rich or poor, Democrat or Republican, and anyone in the LGBT community. They don't care who they kill. No one is safe.

As citizens, we need to unite to combat these

radical Islamic terrorists. We need to use every method at our disposal, which includes common sense, and not political correctness before it is too late.

The FBI needs to create a Suspicious Persons List based on the people they have interviewed for possible terrorist links. This list needs to be supplied to state and local law enforcement agencies. When a person on this list goes to purchase a gun, the FBI would be notified right away and the purchase would be halted until a further investigation is conducted.

Another very important and necessary item is to build a wall between Mexico and the United States. Many don't agree with this, but use common sense. Illegals are pouring across the border, and they are not all innocent families seeking work. Many are criminals and drug dealers who import guns and drugs into our country. And there are also terrorists who blend in with the Hispanics and sneak across the border. A wall would also put a big hurt on illegal drugs being smuggled into this country, which kill our children.

One report, based on Border Patrol data, estimated that a large number of people from middle-east countries come into the United States every year through Mexico. It is a serious problem that can only be solved by building a wall to control illegal entry. If we cannot control our borders, then we will not have a country for long. This is how the Roman Empire fell.

We don't hear much about the Canadian border. There are not hordes of people coming in from Canada yet, but we need to keep an eye on that border, because as time goes on, the terrorists will come from Canada, if they can.

The Radical Islamic terrorists have killed more Muslims than any other group of people. It is time for peaceful freedom-loving American Muslims to come together and put a stop to this radical thinking, wherever they find it. The question is, do Muslims have the will and the courage to do so? Actually, Muslims around the world need to unite against the extremists.

Finally, we have to stop bringing in thousands of refugees from war-torn countries overseas. Our government gives them medical care, food, homes, and money until they can obtain a job, usually working for the government. They are given all these freebies so they can get their feet on the ground, so to speak.

Why can't we provide them safe zones and weapons so they can stay in their homeland, and fight to get their country back? Fight to take back their homes and land that the terrorists took from them.

In my mind, if a person will not stay and fight for his country, then they do not understand the meaning of Patriotism. They have no loyalty to a country. They do not understand the concept of loyalty to one's own nation.

We simply have no idea how many of these refugees will blend into our country or assimilate. We currently have no idea how to vet them to tell how many are radicalized and would pose a threat to our people and country. We cannot absorb thousands of people every year that simply may not fit into our society and way of life. I believe each one should be given a lie detector test.

The United States is far different from the life they know. We have United States immigration laws that should be followed. Currently they are not being enforced. To continue bringing refugees into the U.S. in mass numbers without following the laws, and without proper vetting, is un-American.

It is destroying our values, culture, history, freedoms, and our country as a whole. Simply put, these reckless actions could kill more Americans here at home. Look what open borders are doing to France and Germany. They are having terrorist attacks a few times a month. Do you want to live like that? Do you want to live in fear every day? Do you want to accept terrorist attacks as a way of life?

It's not right giving these refugees everything when we have homeless American Veterans and veterans without jobs. Why aren't our brave veterans given proper medical care, jobs, and homes? They have earned it by serving our country. No foreign refugees are more important than our veterans.

We have enough problems with poor homeless people and joblessness now. We need to take care of our American family first. I have seen too many hungry and homeless people right here in the United States, and you probably have also.

Our country is the best hope for humanity, but it is far from perfect. Let's try to improve our country before we take on the world's problems. When no children are hungry, when there are no homeless, when there are no food lines, when there are no poor, then we as a nation can stand proud. Only then can we do more to help others around the world.

We cannot have an open border and let everyone in who wants to come here. Let's follow our immigration laws and let people in who are worthy to become United States Citizens. Let's use some common sense.

FINAL REMARKS

In conclusion, honest law abiding armed citizens are not the enemy. Terrorists and criminals are the ones to fear. As recently shown by the attack in France, they will use trucks, cars, bombs, and planes to kill us. ***They don't need guns, but we do in order to stop them.*** Making more gun laws or banning guns will accomplish nothing to make us safer. It will only encourage the criminals and terrorists to conduct their evil deeds, unchecked by law abiding Americans.

Who are the people that believe in the 2nd Amendment? We are everybody and we are nobody. We are the people and everyday citizens. We are the farmers, shopkeepers, ministers, business owners, plumbers, and coal miners. We are Americans.

WAKE UP AMERICA … LET'S USE COMMON SENSE!

PART SIX

GUN SELECTION

The following pages discuss gun selection for those new to guns. Please use this guide to help you select a weapon before going to the gun store. This guide is based on the assumption that one wants to purchase a weapon for survival situations.

Introduction

This section will cover gun selection based on what is the most popular ammunition. The gun is your most important asset. However, without ammunition your gun is worthless. What kind of guns should one own? Based on my fifty years of gun experience, the type of gun and caliber is very important for your protection. Guns have only three main purposes, which are hunting, sport shooting, and self-defense. Of course, any of the guns mentioned in this article can be used for hunting or self-defense. The question is, which gun is the best tool for the job? Yes, a gun is a tool just like a hammer or saw.

For those new to guns, I try to explain the differences in a simple manner. When purchasing your first gun, it is a confusing matter to choose the correct one with the large selection on the market. Many people have asked me, what type of gun do I recommend? Where do you go to learn to shoot? I have always advised that gun selection should be based on what is the most available type of ammunition and what you intend to use the gun for.

Common Guns for Hunting

I place guns into two general categories, which are hunting guns and tactical guns, or combat weapons. There may come a time when you will need to hunt for food. There are two common types of hunting guns that can dispatch most animals and that is a 12-gauge shotgun and a .22 caliber rifle or pistol. These two guns allow you good flexibility.

You can use the shotgun for hunting birds, rabbits, deer, or larger animals depending on what type of round you use. In addition, a 12-gauge with slugs or buckshot is a great weapon to use for protection at close range. The one drawback is that shotgun shells are expensive, heavy to carry, and too large to store many of them. Most shotguns are semi-automatic and pump type. They hold five to eight rounds. For the semi-automatic type, you just load and pull the trigger. The faster you pull the trigger, the faster it shoots. The pump needs to be pumped or cocked each time to shoot it. I prefer the semi-auto type because it is faster, easier to clean and use. Double barrel or single shot shotguns are not desirable since you have to reload every time you fire it.

Do not underestimate the .22 caliber rifle or long barrel pistol either, as it can be used on birds and/or small rodents as well as be a tool for self-defense. It is not necessarily the size of the bullet that matters, but it's how well you can shoot. A 22 with hollow point bullets is an easy weapon to use, and you can carry a lot of ammunition since the bullets are so small. You can store 5,000 rounds of this ammo in a desk due to its small size. A rifle has a 200-yard range and a pistol with a 6-inch barrel is good for 50-yards. The 12-gauge shot gun and a .22 caliber rifle are a must to own.

The 22 rifle also comes in pump or semi-auto types. The choice is up to you. As for 22 pistols, there is only one that I will mention and that is the Ruger target model, as it is the best you can buy. My selection for a shotgun is a Remington semi-auto model that handles 2 ¾ inch shells. Purchase a shotgun that has a stock and forearm that is made of modern plastic, as it can stand up better to the elements.

Guns for Self-Defense

There are many types of ammunition used for combat pistols and rifles. The selection of the ammunition is critical to the type of combat rifle or combat pistol you will select for protection. The shotgun and 22 rifle mentioned above are dual-purpose weapons, but are mainly for hunting. The pistols and rifles mentioned below are really the weapons you need for total protection. These are guns that contain 10-round magazines and larger.

What other types of guns do you need to survive? Well, let us first look at what is the most popular type of ammunition on the market to help make our selection. Having enough ammo will be your biggest problem. The fact is, most police and military handguns are 9mm. The 45 caliber and 40 caliber are also popular, but not as common as 9mm luger ammo. The 9mm ammo is also less expensive to purchase.

For rifles, there are only three major types of calibers that are widely used by the police and military. One is the .223 Remington, also known as the 5.56mm NATO round. The other is the AK 47 round 7.62x39, a round used by the military and some police around the world. This is the most popular ammo used by terrorists and gangs because the AK 47 is an inexpensive weapon. The last is the .308 Winchester round or 7.62x51 NATO.

The .223 round is used by the Colt AR 15; or as the military calls it the M16 rifle. It is now named the M4 carbine, and is widely used by our military. There are many different manufactures of the so-called AR 15 design. Some of these AR designs also shoot a 7.62x51 NATO round, which is basically the same as the .308 Winchester, these are called AR 10 rifles. The 7.62x39 and 7.62x51 are not to be confused as they are totally different rounds. The drawback of the 7.62x51 round is the cost, which is higher than the .223. And when you are hauling around 300 rounds, they are also heavier. The 7.62x51 is a long range round and can exceed 800 yards. The .223 round has an effective range of up to 500 yards. You can also purchase an AR-type rifle that will fire the 7.62x39mm round. Colt is one of the best manufactures for AR-type designs, which can be purchased in many different calibers. Several companies also make a .22 caliber AR rifles, such as Colt and the Smith and Wesson M&P 15-22, as well a rifle that fires the 9mm luger round.

The most popular type of ammunition for a pistol is the 9mm luger round. The most common type for a rifle is the .223 Remington, also known as the 5.56mm NATO round. Knowing this, we can select a number of different pistols, rifles, or carbines to use. For this selection, we need to keep in mind durability, ease of cleaning, interchangeability, and ease of use by men or women.

Knowing that we want a handgun that shoots 9mm luger rounds, one should note that most 9mm handguns are semi-automatic design and are not revolvers. Semi-auto means it has a magazine that holds the bullets, and some can hold up to 18 rounds before reloading. There are two handguns that I recommend, which are a Glock and a Springfield Armory model XD. I own both and they are the best dependable handguns on the market. This is not to say there are not other good brands, but based on my shooting experience, buying one of these handguns you cannot go wrong. My favorite, however, is the Glock Model 17 because it is dependable and very easy to clean and repair. Yes, sometimes guns break so you should have some extra parts or a backup gun, if possible. Each gun comes with an assembly manual, and the Glock can be taken apart by just removing the slide and two pins. I have shot thousands of rounds and only had my Glock break one time. The trigger return spring broke and I replaced in 10 minutes with a new one. It is so simple that anyone can work on it. The Glock can be dropped in the mud, run over by a truck, and still shoot. It can be fired under water, and the barrel life is 350,000 rounds, which is more than you will ever shoot in your life time.

Basically, all AR 15-type rifles are the same design and are easy to take apart for cleaning. The models may have different names from different manufactures such as Armalite SPR Mod 1, which is basically the same as a Colt CAR 15 or carbine model of the AR 15 rifle. It pays to buy a good quality rifle from a well-known manufacturer, even if it may cost a little more. Remember, your life may depend on this weapon. If you buy an AR-type rifle then find out what parts you may need to replace by asking the manufacture. I recommend buying two weapons of the same type, this way you have a backup and you do not have to learn about different weapons and the assemblies. Parts between different manufactures are not necessarily interchangeable. The AR 15 can be cleaned in about 10 minutes just by pushing out a pin which opens the rifle up. It is also light weight, so men and women can use it. The recoil is very low, which is important for accurate firing. I recommend the Colt AR 15 .223 as this is a dependable weapon which has been on the market many years.

Some manufactures, such as Colt, have also made CAR 15 carbines that use the pistol 9mm luger round. This is an excellent weapon that has very little recoil but has a limited range of about 100 yards. It is made for close quarter combat situations. Having a CAR 15 9mm is a good choice, since you can use the same ammo as your 9mm handgun.

To summarize, the guns needed are: a 12-gauge shotgun semi-automatic or pump model, a .22 rifle or target pistol, a 9mm handgun, and a .223 (5.56 NATO) AR 15 type rifle. I recommend owing two guns of each type so you have a backup. How much ammo do you need? It is up to you to decide, but the more the better as the gun is worthless without ammunition. If you can only own one or two guns, then the AR 15 rifle and the 9mm Glock are my choices.

Everyone in your family should know how to shoot each type of gun. I suggest one gun for each family member. Gun selection should be made by what each member of the family likes to shoot best. One may like a .22 caliber and one may like a 9mm Glock. Remember, your family is also your Army to help protect each other. So proper training is very important. Do not spare any expense on training. Do not buy cheap unreliable guns.

When you go shooting, do not purchase reloads. Reloads are made with used shell casings. Reloads can misfire and be very dirty, which can jam up your gun. Buy new ammo as it is clean and more accurate.

Gun Safety

If you have no experience with guns then it is suggested that you learn by going to your local gun store or shooting range and take lessons from a good instructor. If you have a friend who shoots, go with him to the range your first time and check it out. The National Rifle Association or NRA is a valuable resource to use for this learning process. Shooters are friendly people and they are always happy to help out a beginner.

The NRA has safety rules, which you can find listed online. It is a must to read the NRA safety rules. The worst thing you can do is buy a gun and not know how to use it or even load it. If you are faced with a threat to your life or that of your family, then you better know how to use the weapon with some degree of skill. The more skillful you are, the better your chance of survival will be. We are talking life and death situations that require split-second decisions on your part, so shooting practice is very necessary. Join a local shooting club to hone your skills.

I stress, do not buy a gun just to own one. Do not buy a gun if you will never practice or shoot it. How much practice do you need? Based on my experience, the more the better, but I think shooting your weapon at least three hours per month is necessary to become a good shot and learn everything about your gun. I know many people who shoot two hours or more a week. I also stress that one should take combat shooting lessons at a gun school such as Gun Sight. They will train you in Home Defense, Vehicle Defense, Tactical Rifle, Pistol, and Shotgun use. Be the best you can be as learning to shoot is more than just going to the range and pulling the trigger.

Above all, be a safe shooter and follow the NRA safety rules. When not in use, keep your guns locked up so kids cannot access them and they cannot be stolen from you. I strongly suggest a gun safe to store your guns and ammo as it will give you peace of mind. You can also keep other valuables in the safe. Shooting can be a great hobby providing much enjoyment and fun for the whole family.

Shoot safe and shoot straight.

PART SEVEN

THE BILL OF RIGHTS

Amendment I

Congress shall make no law respecting an establishment of religion, or prohibiting the free exercise thereof; or abridging the freedom of speech, or of the press; or the right of the people peaceably to assemble, and to petition the government for a redress of grievances.

Amendment II

A well regulated Militia, being necessary to the security of a free State, the right of the people to keep and bear Arms, shall not be infringed.

Amendment III

No soldier shall, in time of peace be quartered in any house, without the consent of the owner, nor in time of war, but in a manner to be prescribed by law.

Amendment IV

The right of the people to be secure in their persons, houses, papers, and effects, against unreasonable searches and seizures, shall not be violated, and no warrants shall issue, but upon probable cause, supported by oath or affirmation, and particularly describing the place to be searched, and the persons or things to be seized.

Amendment V

No person shall be held to answer for a capital, or otherwise infamous crime, unless on a presentment or indictment of a grand jury, except in cases arising in the land or naval forces, or in the militia, when in actual service in time of war or public danger; nor shall any person be subject for the same offense to be twice put in jeopardy of life or limb; nor shall be compelled in any criminal case to be a witness against himself, nor be deprived of life, liberty, or property, without due process of law; nor shall private property be taken for public use, without just compensation.

Amendment VI

In all criminal prosecutions, the accused shall enjoy the right to a speedy and public trial, by an impartial jury of the state and district wherein the crime shall have been committed, which district shall have been previously ascertained by law, and to be informed of the nature and cause of the accusation; to be confronted with the witnesses against him; to have compulsory process for obtaining witnesses in his favor, and to have the assistance of counsel for his defense.

Amendment VII

In suits at common law, where the value in controversy shall exceed twenty dollars, the right of trial by jury shall be preserved, and no fact tried by a jury, shall be otherwise reexamined in any court of the United States, than according to the rules of the common law.

Amendment VIII
Excessive bail shall not be required, nor excessive fines imposed, nor cruel and unusual punishments inflicted.

Amendment IX
The enumeration in the Constitution, of certain rights, shall not be construed to deny or disparage others retained by the people.

Amendment X
The powers not delegated to the United States by the Constitution, nor prohibited by it to the states, are reserved to the states respectively, or to the people.

THOMAS H. WARD

REFERENCES

https://www.google.com/#q=define+milita

www.guncite.com/gc2ndmea.html

http://www.history.com/topics/american-revolution/battles-of-lexington-and-concord

https://en.wikipedia.org/wiki/Battles_of_Lexington_and_Concord

http://www.ushistory.org/us/11c.asp

http://www.americanthinker.com/articles/2016/04/what_does_the_second_amendment_mean.html

http://tenthamendmentcenter.com/2014/09/22/2nd-amendment-original-meaning-and-purpose/

https://en.wikipedia.org/wiki/2016_**Orlando**_nightclub_**shooting**

 www.breitbart.com/tech/2016/06/30/wikipedia-removes-orlando-shooting-islamist-terror-attack-list/

http://hotair.com/archives/2016/06/12/multiple-casualties-in-orlando-from-act-of-terrorism-at-night-club/

www.cnn.com/2016/06/12/us/**orlando**-nightclub-shooting/

www.cnn.com/2016/06/12/us/**orlando**-shooting-what-we-know/

https://en.wikipedia.org/wiki/2015_**San_Bernardino_attack**

www.latimes.com/.../la-me-**san-bernardino**-shooting-**terror**-investig

http://www.cnn.com/specials/san-bernardino-shooting

https://en.wikipedia.org/wiki/2009_**Fort_Hood**_shooting

http://www.cbsnews.com/feature/tragedy-at-fort-hood/

www.history.com/.../army-major-kills-13-people-in-**fort-hood**-shooting-spree

https://en.wikipedia.org/wiki/2014_Fort_Hood_shooting

https://en.wikipedia.org/wiki/**Boston**_Marathon_**bombing**

www.history.com/topics/**boston**-marathon-**bombings**

https://www.britannica.com/event/Boston-Marathon-bombing-of-2013

https://en.wikipedia.org/wiki/Terrorist_Screening_Database

https://en.wikipedia.org/wiki/**Internment**_of_Japanese_**Americans**

https://en.wikipedia.org/wiki/**Internment**_of_German_**Americans**

https://home.nra.org/

http://training.nra.org/nra-gun-safety-rules.aspx

https://www.billofrightsinstitute.org/founding-documents/bill-of-rights/

ABOUT THE AUTHOR

You are probably wondering who I am and what makes me qualified to write about guns. Not much, other than my fifty plus years of gun experience, so I know more than most people. Not much, other than I've been in dangerous situations more than once in my life, where a weapon was the only thing between me and possible death. So I know what it feels like. Until you have been put in that situation, you have no idea what it is like.

I do know guns. I spent fifty years honing my skills. I know how to use them in life or death situations, and not just shooting at a bull's-eye target. I have been trained by some of the best in the use of rifles, shotguns, and handguns.

I'm a nobody, no hero, never been in the military, or fought in a war. I did serve my country during the Vietnam time period in another capacity, which required a DOD (Department of Defense) secret clearance and a AEC (Atomic Energy Commission) classified clearance. The government didn't hand out those clearances to just anybody in those days. It was a big deal to pass the FBI security checks. It was a big deal to pass a lie detector screening.

So, who else is better suited to talk about guns? I am sure there are many out there. The police and military for sure could talk about guns. But, since I am a writer, I decided to have my thoughts published in this thought-provoking book of common sense.

OTHER BOOKS BY
THOMAS H. WARD

To Contact the author:

Visit his website: www.ThomasHWardBooks.com

Or by email: thomashward46@gmail.com

Visit Thomas H. Ward's Amazon Author Page:

www.ingramcontent.com/pod-product-compliance
Lightning Source LLC
Chambersburg PA
CBHW050532280326
41933CB00011B/1554